CLIFF FOR THE RECORD

CLIFF

FOR THE
RECORD

STEVE TURNER

HarperCollins*Publishers*

HarperCollins*Publishers*
77–85 Fulham Palace Road, London W6 8JB
First published in 1997 by
HarperCollins*Publishers*

Text Copyright ©1997 Steve Turner
10 9 8 7 6 5 4 3 2 1

A catalogue record for this book is
available from the British Library

0 551 03081 X

Printed and bound in Italy by
New Interlitho Italia S.P.A.

CONTENTS

SIR CLIFF RICHARD

I'm always amazed that, despite all that's been written and printed about me and my career over the years, there still seems to be something new to share.

I guess that, if anyone has the ability to dig out the obscure and previously unseen, it's Steve Turner. Where he's found some of these pictures, I've no idea. I'd long since forgotten them! Well done, Steve - you've intrigued me!

Cliff Richard

Sir Cliff Richard

INTRODUCTION

The focus of this book is the 40 years of Cliff's performing career which began in September 1957 when he took over as the vocalist for the Dick Teague Skiffle Group. Some earlier shots have been included to set the scene.

The aim has been to document as many of the key events of Cliff's career as would fit in the space available. Photos taken by professional photographers have been supplemented with personal snaps supplied by friends and colleagues.

This has meant sifting through thousands of prints, contact sheets and transparencies and I have tried, wherever possible, to select images that haven't been widely used.

Few British people can have been as extensively photographed as Cliff. Since his first recording, made when he was still 17 years old, he has been under the constant scrutiny of press cameras.

Looking through the Cliff Richard files of photographic agencies led me to wonder what the man did when he wasn't being photographed. It was as if he had lived his whole life under surveillance. There are pictures of Cliff sleeping in bed, combing his hair, shaving and dressing. There are pictures of him driving, eating, drinking and even shopping for shoes.

The other recurring thought was that Cliff was made for the camera. Everything about the composition of his face, his build and even the texture of his hair was a blessing to photographers. He never seemed to take a bad picture.

He might have occasionally been out of focus or out of shot but he never revealed a bad angle.

'I don't really think that I'm good looking,' he once told me. 'I just think that some people have faces that photograph well.'

Most of us would be copious collectors of our own memorabilia if we had led as rich a life as Cliff. Our shelves would be groaning under the weight of scrapbooks and files and our walls would be covered with portraits of us shaking hands with the rich and famous. But Cliff remains remarkably unfazed by all that has happened to him.

When I asked him if he had any photographs for my 1993 book, *Cliff Richard: The Biography,* he surprised me by telling me that he had nothing. 'I've never collected things like that,' he said. 'I don't even have any press cuttings or a complete collection of my own records. I certainly don't have any original copies of my albums and singles.'

This is probably the way it should be. It's the performer's job to focus on the future and it's the fan's role to reminisce about the past.

STEVE TURNER 1997

THE FIFTIES '50s

After only a year of performing Cliff was awarded a recording contract with Columbia Records, and his first single 'Move It' reached the Top Twenty in September 1958.

Jack Good's weekly television show *Oh Boy!* played an important part in this swift transition. Cliff was a regular guest and Good coached him in stagecraft, turning the shy boy from Cheshunt into a 'smouldering' rock 'n' roll star who some feared was a 'crude exhibitionist' who was far too 'vulgar' to be seen on television.

Months of one-nighters followed, accompanied by unprecedented scenes of fan mayhem. His original Drifters were soon replaced by Hank Marvin, Bruce Welch, Jet Harris and Tony Meehan, who became collectively known as the Shadows.

Within twelve months he starred in two films, *Serious Charge* and *Expresso Bongo*, made his debut in pantomime and appeared on Britain's most watched television entertainment show, *Sunday Night At The London Palladium*.

During the '50s Cliff released six singles, three extended plays and two albums. His last two singles of 1959, 'Living Doll' and 'Travellin' Light', both topped the charts and sold in excess of 1.5 million copies each.

In 1958 the readers of *New Musical Express* voted Cliff 'favourite new singer'. Twelve months later they voted him 'best male artist'.

MBIA

MADE IN GT. BRITA

45-DB 4178

MOVE IT!
(Samwell)
CLIFF RICHARD
and the Drifters

ABOVE: Coronation Day, June 1953. The children of Hargreaves Close, Cheshunt, including Cliff (centre row, third from right), celebrate in the street.

RIGHT: December 1956. Cliff (second from left) as Bob Cratchit in a school production of *A Christmas Carol*.

ABOVE: July 1956. Cliff (far left) makes his singing debut with the Quintones at the Holy Trinity School, Waltham Cross.

BELOW. The Dick Teague Skiffle Group, December 1957. 'One of my favourite photos of the early days. I had the curly lip and looked very Elvis-ish.'

ABOVE: February 1958. Practising in the kitchen of the family home in Cheshunt.

LEFT: The guitars used by the Drifters, proudly lined up for their own group photograph.

ABOVE: Photographed on the
Bury Green Estate, Cheshunt,
close to his council house home.

ABOVE: The original Drifters line-up featuring Cliff and Norman Mitham (guitars) and Terry Smart (drums).

Admit ONE to
THE TUDOR HALL, Hoddesdon
Friday, June 27th, 1958 at 8 p.m.

MISSIN LINKS
and DRIFTERS

RHYTHM
GROUPS

Jiving Competition (prizes)

Bar applied for

TICKET 3/6

50s

ABOVE: The Drifters with new member Ian 'Sammy' Samwell (seated) playing at the 2I's coffee bar, Soho.

LEFT: Backstage at the Kilburn State, on 25 May 1958. 'Jerry Lee Lewis was the first famous person I had ever met. We were all overwhelmed.'

ABOVE: When Norman Mitham left, the Drifters became a trio again with Terry Smart, Cliff and Sammy Samwell.

RIGHT: Cliff's debut single was written by Samwell while travelling on a Green Line bus from London Colney to Cheshunt.

'50s

TOP LEFT: August 1958. The Drifters performing at the Rock 'n' Roll Ballroom, Butlin's Holiday Camp, Clacton.

LEFT BOTTOM: Cliff with fellow Butlin's entertainer Henri Rouah.

LEFT: Drifters Terry Smart and Ian Samwell (bottom), with manager John Foster and friend.

BELOW: Third from left is Jan Vane, the founder of the original Cliff Richard Fan Club.

'50s

LEFT AND ABOVE: The Drifters and manager John Foster between shows at Butlin's.

ABOVE: Cliff's first publicity
shot. 'It was taken by an EMI
photographer in the corner of
Studio 2 at Abbey Road.'

LEFT TOP: **Cliff, his sister Donna and Terry Smart listen to the American record releases on the radiogram.**

LEFT, BOTTOM LEFT: **Cliff and Terry watched by Cliff's parents.**

LEFT, BOTTOM RIGHT: **A family meal with father at the head of the table.**

RIGHT: **Cliff's parents, Rodger and Dorothy Webb.**

BELOW: **Cliff with a cousin, an uncle and his sister Jackie (right).**

LEFT: On the brink of fame, Cliff poses with his mother at home.

BELOW: 'I mimed to Elvis's records and tried to get my hair right.'

'50s

ABOVE: With Rick Richards of the Worried Men, at the 2I's coffee bar, just prior to Cliff's 1958 tour with the Kalin Twins.

RIGHT: After changing his name from Harry Webb, Cliff sent this jokey postcard to Rick Richards.

CLIFF RICHARD
COLUMBIA RECORDS

Photo: Flair

LEFT: **16 November 1958. On stage at the Trocadero, Elephant and Castle, London.**

BELOW: **In action on his first tour of Britain.**

TOP TWENTY

Week ending: October 18th				
Last Week	This Week	Title		Artist
1	1	Stupid Cupid / Carolina Moon		Connie Francis
2	2	Move It		Cliff Richard
2	3	King Creole		Elvis Presley
4	4	Born Too Late		Poni-Tails
5	5	Bird Dog		Everly Bro...
6	6	Come Prima / Volare		Marino M...
11	7	A Certain Smile		Johnny...
	8			

ABOVE: **Photographed by Rick Richards at the 2I's coffee bar.**

'50s

ABOVE: 'I wore a black shirt, pink tie and pink jacket. It was Teddy Boyish – slightly draped. I also had a yellow jacket.'

ABOVE: **1 December 1958.**
Backstage at the Finsbury Park
Empire.

'50^s

'50s

BELOW: In the dressing room during the filming of the *Oh Boy!* television show, with his friend and confidante Cherry Wainer.

boyfriend of the week ♡ Cliff

ABOVE: 'I realized early on that the fans want to own you, and I was happy about that'.

ABOVE: **Cliff in the role of Curly Thompson with Andrew Ray in the film *Serious Charge*.**

RIGHT: **'I loved the screaming. In fact, I felt as though I'd failed if I didn't get a scream or two.'**

'50s

TOP: Cliff with his friend and mentor Jack Good, creator of *Oh Boy!*.

ABOVE: May 1959. An *Oh Boy!* line-up featuring Cliff with the Dallas Boys, Marty Wilde, Billy Fury and Cherry Wainer.

'50^s

**Trying on Elvis for size during a
recording for *Oh Boy!*.**

LEFT: By early 1959 the Drifters consisted of Hank Marvin (lead guitar), Jet Harris (bass), Bruce Welch (rhythm guitar) and Tony Meehan (drums).

ABOVE: **28 April 1959. Recording 'Living Doll' at Abbey Road Studios.**

rthur Howes
presents

Oh Boy !

ODEON
Tottenham Ct. Road
W.1.

* *

SUNDAY,
3rd MAY, 1959

THE
CLIFF RICHARD
SHOW

Souvenir
Programme

OPPOSITE: Signing autographs outside the Shepherds Bush Empire.

LEFT: Cliff and the Drifters with new manager Tito Burns.

BELOW: 'Clocking in' at the London Palladium.

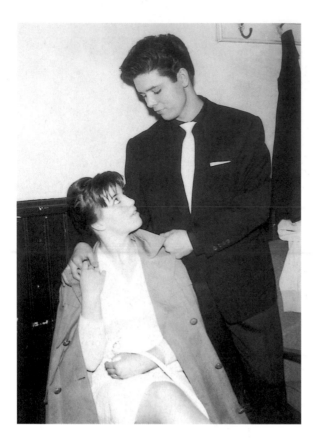

ABOVE: A reassuring touch for
Carol Costa, wife of Jet Harris,
pregnant with her first child.

'50

ABOVE: In a television studio dressing room with Hollywood movie star Jayne Mansfield.

'50^s

ABOVE AND LEFT: **Filming**
Expresso Bongo at Shepperton
Studios. Cliff played the part of
rising rock 'n' roll star Bongo
Herbert.

ABOVE: 4 February 1959.
Recovering after a riot broke up
his concert at the Lyceum in
London.

LEFT: **June 1959. With his friend Pam on holiday in Viareggio, Italy.**

BELOW: **On the beach in Italy with Ronnie Ernstone, the friend who taught him how to drive.**

50ˢ

'50s

ABOVE: Cliff and the Drifters recording the album *Cliff* in front of an invited audience.

LEFT: After seeing American group the Treniers at the Trocadero, Elephant and Castle, the Drifters developed a step routine.

THE SIXTIES '60s

For the first half of the '60s Cliff dominated the British charts with a series of million-selling singles, while simultaneously breaking cinema box office records with *The Young Ones*, *Summer Holiday* and *Wonderful Life*. With the Shadows he toured extensively in Britain and Europe and made his first visits to Australia, South Africa, America and Canada.

However, following the death of his father he began to re-evaluate his life and over a period of time this led to his Christian conversion.

In the summer of 1966 he was a platform guest at a London meeting featuring the American evangelist Billy Graham. It was here that he made the first public declaration of his new-found faith.

His position as Britain's leading pop phenomenon had by now been usurped by the likes of the Beatles and the Rolling Stones but, in his frame of mind, Cliff didn't seem to mind.

A period of uncertainty followed during which he agonized over the best way to use his talents. He briefly considered becoming a religious education teacher but came to realize that music was his special talent and found ways to express his beliefs through gospel songs.

Between December 1965 and March 1969 he virtually abandoned touring, his major dates being seasons at the Palladium, Talk of the Town and Butlin's.

'60s

ABOVE: Touring America,
January 1960. Cliff meets fans,
the rest of the tour freeze on the
bus. Note the slush on the floor!

RIGHT: Jet and Hank with Freddy
Cannon (left) and Johnny Paris
of Johnny and the Hurricanes
(right).

ABOVE: Cliff tests out Jack Good inspired moves in the land of Elvis.

ABOVE RIGHT: Sammy and Jet hang up their clothes properly.

RIGHT: Jet tests out a cool porkpie hat purchased in New York.

FAR RIGHT: And then he tests out a hotel bed.

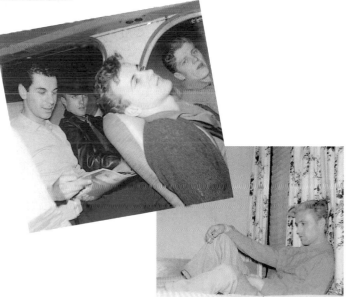

RIGHT: An unusual photograph showing Cliff with Jet Harris and his wife Carol Costa. Cliff was soon to become involved with Carol. 'Brief encounter though it was, it was certainly a growing up experience for me.'

TOP: Cliff signs a contract under the watchful eye of his parents and manager Tito Burns.

ABOVE: A party in Hounslow attended by Cliff, Jet Harris, Carol Costa and Hank Marvin.

'60s

RIGHT: December 1960. Backstage at the London Palladium with *Stars In Your Eyes* line-up Billy Dainty, Russ Conway, Joan Regan, Des O'Connor, David Kossoff and Edmund Hockridge.

BELOW: Rehearsing lines for *The Young Ones* with Melvyn Hayes, Annette Robinson, Carole Gray and Teddy Green.

ABOVE: At Elstree Studios with his leading lady Carole Gray while filming *The Young Ones*.

BELOW: 'After having gone through the pink jackets and all that we were very much into being accepted by the mums and dads.'

CLIFF FOR THE RECORD

'60s

LEFT: August 1961. On the beach at Blackpool during a season at the Opera House.

ABOVE: Another day, another town, another pair of swimming trunks.

RIGHT: A tribute single recorded by Don Lang, star of TV programme *6:5 Special*.

They Call Him Cliff

Words and Music by Gordon Langhorn, Bill Crompton, Morgan Jones.

Music of all Music Dealers and of the Copyright Owners—Mills Music Ltd., Mills House, Denmark Street, London, W.C.2.

I know a boy who can really move it,
I know a guy who is dynamite,
He's got a livin' doll 'round ev'ry corner,
But he keeps on travellin' light.

Chorus
THEY CALL HIM CLIFF.
Ev'ry time he takes a microphone in his hand,
a-well, a-well, a-well, he shakes a hip,
Moves a fingertip,
And they scream and they shout,
And they know just what it's all about,
'Cos there ain't another boy who can move it
around like Cliff.

He sings a song 'bout a high-class baby.
He jumps around like a crackerjack,
And when he starts a-feelin' kind-a moody
Well, there ain't no turnin' back.

He's got a kick like Expresso bongo.
But he's as cool as a watercress,
And all the chicks go crazy when they listen
To that voice in the wilderness.

Recorded by
DON LANG
on H.M.V. Pop714

LEFT: **13 December 1961. With his mother and Carole Gray at the gala premiere of *The Young Ones* in London.**

TODAY

'60s

ABOVE: October 1961. A nervous looking Cliff, celebrating his 21st birthday, listens to a presentation speech by EMI Chairman, Sir Joseph Lockwood.

'60s

RIGHT: **May 1962. Bruce Welch and Cliff filming *Summer Holiday* in Athens.**

BELOW: **The first change in the Shadows came when drummer Tony Meehan left and was replaced by Brian Bennett.**

BELOW: *Summer Holiday* director Peter Yates with Cliff and Lauri Peters.

RIGHT: *Summer Holiday* producer Kenneth Harper (far right), and future *Midnight Cowboy* star Jon Voight to the left of Cliff. Voight was then married to Lauri Peters.

Cliff crosses Times Square with road manager Mike Conlin, shops at Macy's department store and meets TV host Ed Sullivan.

'60s

CLIFF FOR THE RECORD 83

'60s

RIGHT: 11 January 1963. Watching TV at manager Peter Gormley's flat, after crowds prevented him attending the premiere of *Summer Holiday*.

ABOVE: With Jackie Irving, the dancer who became his girlfriend in 1961 and who later married Adam Faith. 'A stunning looking girl and a smashing person.'

'60s

ABOVE: January 1963. On tour in South Africa.

LEFT: With Jackie Irving. 'I found myself more attracted to her than anyone else and spent more time with her.'

LEFT: April 1963. In Sitges, Spain. John Lennon and Beatles manager Brian Epstein were staying at the same hotel as Cliff and the Shadows.

ABOVE: With Frank Ifield, the Australian singer with whom he shared a manager.

BELOW: Recording the album *When In Spain* in Barcelona. Cliff discusses details with producer Norrie Paramor. Engineer Malcolm Addey sits at the desk with Cliff's manager Peter Gormley.

'60

RIGHT: The second change in the Shadows came when Jet Harris was replaced by Brian 'Licorice' Locking.

BELOW: A rare shot of Cliff in spectacles during a tour of Britain in 1963.

ABOVE: Cliff's first 'pop star mansion' in Upper Nazeing, Essex, purchased in 1963.

RIGHT: Peter Gormley, the manager who guided his career from 1961 until the early '80s.

'60s

The first major threat to Cliff's career came in 1963 when Beatlemania broke out in Britain. The smart Brylcreemed look was soon to be on its way out.

LEFT TOP: **Eating with the cast
of** *Wonderful Life* **including
Melvyn Hayes and Una Stubbs.**

LEFT AND ABOVE: **April 1964.
The third change in the
Shadows came when John
Rostill replaced Licorice Locking.**

ABOVE AND RIGHT: During 1964 Cliff played over 45 theatre dates throughout Britain.

'60s

ABOVE: The welcomes at airports that Cliff received in countries like South Africa were every bit as wild as Beatlemania.

'60s

Exteriors for *Wonderful Life* were
filmed in the Canary Islands.
The original setting was to have
been Mexico.

ABOVE: Rehearsing lines with Una Stubbs. 'When we were filming we were very, very close.'

RIGHT: Posing for Christmas photos in October 1964.

ABOVE: 'Susan Hampshire would fill her mouth with cotton wool because she thought she was too thin for the part.'

'60s

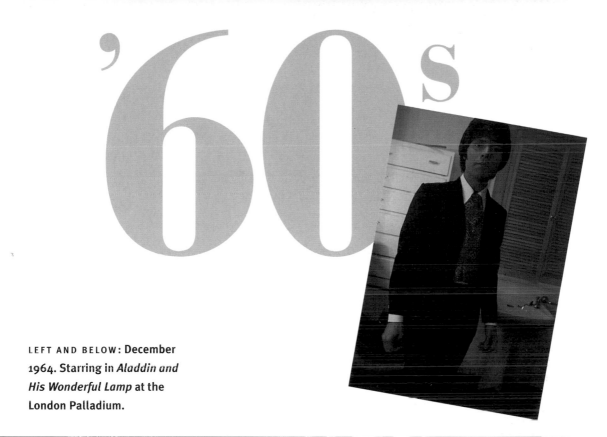

LEFT AND BELOW: December 1964. Starring in *Aladdin and His Wonderful Lamp* at the London Palladium.

'60s

May 1966. A photo call for Cliff and Viviane Ventura, his co-star in *Finders Keepers*.

'60s

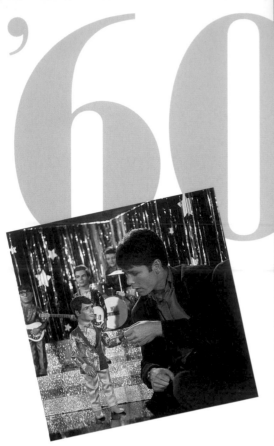

ABOVE: On the set of
Thunderbirds Are Go with
marionettes of himself and
the Shadows.

ABOVE: October 1967. With the future Archbishop of Canterbury, Dr Donald Coggan.

'60s

RIGHT: The first evangelistic pamphlet to bear Cliff's name.

BELOW: With American evangelist Billy Graham on the set of the film *Two A Penny*.

’**60**’

It's 1968 and Cliff celebrates his
first decade in show business.

'60s

LEFT: At home in Totteridge, North London, in the house that he shared with Tear Fund worker Bill Latham (later to become his charity manager) and Bill's mother Mamie.

LEFT: **Eurovision 1968. Cliff sang 'Congratulations' and lost out to the Spanish entry 'La La La'.**

BELOW: **With Cilla Black and 'Congratulations' writers Phil Coulter and Bill Martin.**

ABOVE: On the set of *Two A Penny* with Ann Holloway, Dora Bryan and Billy Graham.

LEFT: The clean college boy look that coincided with Cliff's emergence as a committed Christian.

RIGHT: Performing a sketch with Una Stubbs and Hank Marvin for his BBC TV series *It's Cliff Richard*.

ABOVE: On stage with the Settlers: Mike Jones, Cindy Kent and John Fyffe.

RIGHT: August 1968. Being entertained in Burbank, California, while on holiday.

BELOW: August 1966. Setting off for a holiday in Portugal.

'60s

ABOVE: Christmas 1965. In a
party mood at the home of Bill
Latham.

CLIFF FOR THE RECORD 123

'60s

THE SEVENTIES '70s

The early '70s was the low point of Cliff's recording career. It saw the release of his first single not to chart ('Brand New Day'), his worst selling single ('It's Only Me You've Left Behind') and his first year without a hit (1975).

His energies were directed towards television, where he hosted three series of *It's Cliff Richard* for the BBC, and the theatre where he acted in the plays *Five Finger Exercise* and *The Potting Shed*.

When he toured it was increasingly as a cabaret artist, singing his back catalogue to diners at the Batley Variety Club in Yorkshire, the Fiesta in Sheffield or the Golden Garter in Manchester.

But, just as it appeared that he had run out of steam, he surprised everyone by coming back with the singles 'Miss You Nights' and 'Devil Woman', from the album *I'm Nearly Famous*. 'Devil Woman' gave Cliff his first American Top Ten hit and the album was his first Top Five entry in Britain since *Wonderful Life* in 1964.

I'm Nearly Famous gave Cliff credibility as an album artist and restored his chart fortunes. It was followed by *Every Face Tell A Story*, *Green Light* and *Rock 'n' Roll Juvenile* all of which were backed up by a new state-of-the-art stage show and a permanent touring band.

Cliff ended the decade with 'We Don't Talk Anymore', his best-selling single ever, which was written by one of his band members, Australian Alan Tarney.

ABOVE: Cliff didn't get into his
long hair and paisley shirt
period until the early '70s.

RIGHT: With resident *Top of the
Pops* dancers Pan's People.

ABOVE: After the Shadows came Marvin, Welch and Farrar, with future *Heathcliff* composer John Farrar second from right.

LEFT: With Olivia Newton-John. 'I never got the romantic vibe from her and yet felt totally comfortable and would like to feel that she felt the same way about me.'

'70s

'70s

In 1973 Cliff moved to a £70,000 house in Weybridge, Surrey.

ABOVE: November 1973. Visiting
a refugee camp in Bangladesh
with Tear Fund worker Liz
Hutchison.

RIGHT: Three years later he
returned to examine the progress
made by aid programmes.

BELOW: June 1973. With Debbie Watling during the filming of *Take Me High*.

RIGHT: With Mother Teresa in Calcutta, the city that he and his family left in 1948.

'70s

ABOVE: **Singing to the residents of a Calcutta hostel for the homeless.**

LEFT: **Promotional photograph from April 1975.**

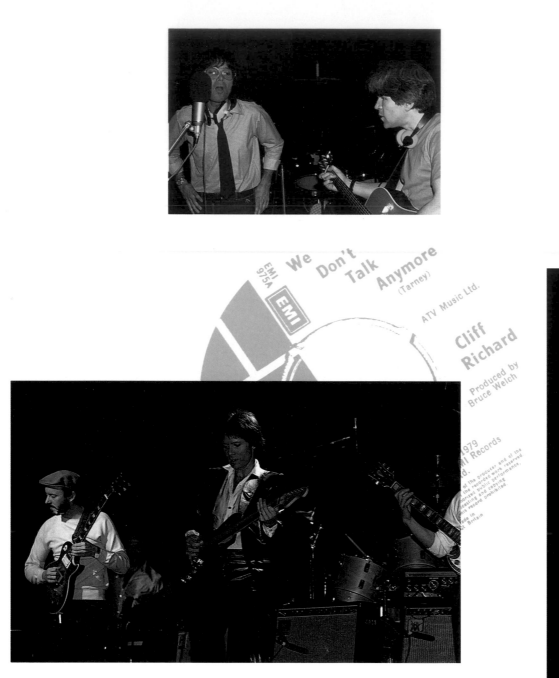

TOP: In the studio with Alan Tarney, the producer and writer who would help re-launch his record career in the '70s.

ABOVE AND RIGHT: On the road promoting 'We Don't Talk Anymore' in 1979.

'70s

THE EIGHTIES '80s

The '80s was Cliff's best decade ever for albums. Following on the success of 'We Don't Talk Anymore', he formed a close partnership with Alan Tarney who produced and played a major writing role in *I'm No Hero*, *Wired For Sound*, *Always Guaranteed* and *Stronger*, all of which made the Top Ten.

He was also scoring with singles. 'Carrie', 'Dreamin'' and 'Daddy's Home' all sold over a million copies. His credibility was increased by collaborations with Van Morrison ('Whenever God Shines His Light'), The Young Ones ('Livin' Doll') and the production team of Stock, Aitken & Waterman ('I Just Don't Have the Heart').

When he wasn't on stage or in the studio he could be found on the tennis court. His involvement with the sport led to a two-year romantic involvement with tennis player Sue Barker, much to the joy of the tabloid press.

In April 1986 he opened in London's West End in the musical *Time*. Although the production was savaged by theatre critics, Cliff stayed with it for a year and drew in an audience of over 700,000.

Cliff had started the '80s by being awarded the OBE and he closed it with his most ambitious performance ever – two nights at Wembley Stadium with the Shadows and the cast of *Oh Boy!* as the main support acts. The combined audience was in excess of 144,000. Only Michael Jackson, Madonna, Bruce Springsteen, Genesis and the Rolling Stones had ever equalled or surpassed this achievement at Wembley.

'80s

LEFT: **3 April 1981. A sound-check in Philadelphia during his fourth tour of America.**

RIGHT: **Back together with Jack Good in New York.**

BELOW: **On his way to a concert in Baltimore, Maryland.**

ABOVE: December 1981. A duet with one of his rock 'n' roll idols, Phil Everly.

RIGHT: Recreating the '50s for BBC TV at the Hard Rock Cafe, London.

TOP RIGHT: December 1981. Together with the Drifters for the first time in 22 years. From left to right: Sammy Samwell, Norman Mitham, Terry Smart and Cliff.

'80s

'80s

LEFT: On stage for a rock 'n' roll concert at the Odeon, Hammersmlth, which was filmed by the BBC.

ABOVE: **His brief romance with tennis player Sue Barker surprised his fans and excited the media.**

RIGHT: **The arrival at Heathrow that alerted the fans.**

FAR RIGHT: **Watching tennis at Wimbledon.**

'80s

'80s

ABOVE: Visiting Haiti on behalf of Tear Fund. The trip inspired Cliff to write two new songs.

ABOVE: **March 1980. Custard pie treatment in South Africa from members of the tour.**

'80s

ABOVE: **With fellow Brit rockers Paul Young, Rod Stewart, George Michael and Ronnie Wood.**

LEFT: **On stage in Montreux, Switzerland, 1984.**

ABOVE: His band of the early '80s. Top row, left to right: Stu Calver (backing vocals), Alan Park (keyboards), Mark Griffiths (bass), John Clark (lead guitar), Dave Cooke (keyboards). Bottom row, left to right: Tony Rivers and John Perry (backing vocals), Graham Jarvis (drums) and Mart Jenner (rhythm guitar).

'80s

'80s

ABOVE: Summer 1987. A Portuguese holiday with his old friends Bill Latham, Glyn McAuley and David Rivett.

BELOW: April 1988. With his co-stars in the musical *Time*: Jodie Wilson, Dawn Hope and Maria Ventura.

ABOVE: Cliff with his mother,
and sisters Joan (left) and
Donna (right).

LEFT: 15 June 1987. Speaking to
Prince Edward during the filming of *It's A Royal Knockout*.

'80s

LEFT: **Summer 1987. On the Thames promoting his new album** *Always Guaranteed.*

RIGHT: **Thirty years in show business and he still has to comb his own hair.**

'80s

RIGHT: June 1989. Preparing for 'The Event', his most ambitious concert ever.

BELOW: Relaxing at his villa in Portugal. Cliff had been one of the first Brits to buy a villa on the Algarve in the early '60s.

ABOVE: Reunited at 'The Event' with former Shadows Jet Harris (left) and Tony Meehan (right). It was an emotional occasion for everyone involved.

0ˢ

'80s

'It was the biggest crowd I'd ever
sung to. I was nervous. I'd never
done anything quite like it before.'

'80s

RIGHT: 30 October 1989.
Promoting *Stronger*, his final
album of the '80s.

THE NINETIES '90s

Touring in the '90s is a relaxed affair compared to the one-nighters and package tours of earlier decades. Cliff now has the size of audience to enable him to settle into a large venue such as Birmingham's NEC for residencies of up to two weeks.

His experience with the 'Almost Guaranteed' and 'Access All Areas' tours between 1990 and 1992, during which he broke attendance records at London's Wembley Arena (18 nights, 216,000 people), encouraged him to develop the idea of touring a musical based on Emily Brönte's *Wuthering Heights*.

He engaged John Farrar to compose the music and Tim Rice to write the lyrics, planning to take it on the road in the autumn of 1994. The songs were completed on time but not the production and so the premiere was postponed and the tour substituted by 'The Hit List', a show featuring all of his singles to reach the Top Five. *Heathcliff* finally opened in 1996 to harsh reviews and huge crowds.

His life is now happily divided between work and his two homes in Weybridge, Surrey, and the Algarve, Portugal. He continues with his passion for tennis and, in 1992, took up winter skiing.

In 1995, *The Guinness Book of Records* recorded that Cliff had now had the most hit singles in the British charts (110). The same year he was invited to perform at the VE celebrations outside Buckingham Palace and on 25 October he received his knighthood, the first pop star ever to do so.

'90s

14 May 1992. With Olivia
Newton-John at the World Music
Awards, Monaco.

ABOVE AND RIGHT: **Visiting
Tear Fund projects in Uganda.
Cliff says that his experiences
travelling in developing countries
have helped to bring a sense of
perspective to his life.**

'90ˢ

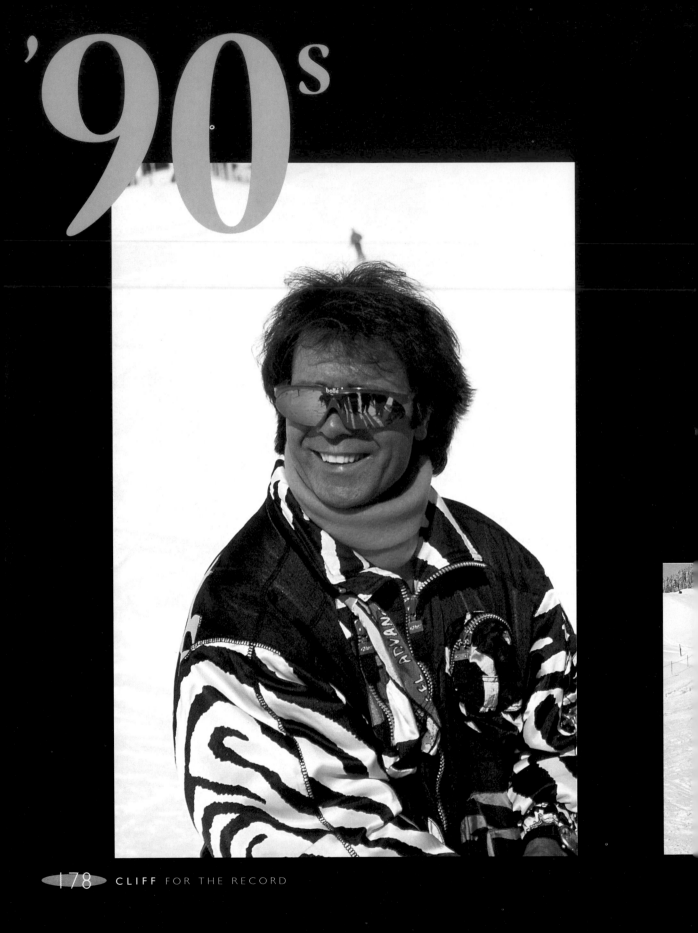

'**90**ˢ

ABOVE: Tennis became a serious part of his life after meeting Sue Barker. He later became involved in encouraging the sport in schools and in organizing Pro-Am tournaments.

LEFT: Skiing in Lech, Austria. Although he was a late starter, he attacked the sport with his typical passion.

ABOVE: **With his Rolls Royce Silver Shadow, which was recently replaced by a Bentley Continental.**

RIGHT: **On the 'Access All Areas' tour in 1992. Staging, lighting and choreography have become increasingly important in Cliff's shows.**

'90s

LEFT: **25 October 1995. With his sisters Donna, Joan and Jackie at Buckingham Palace after receiving his knighthood.**

'90s

ABOVE: **Meeting John Major, then Prime Minister, and his wife Norma.**

LEFT: **16 December 1991. With Diana, Princess of Wales.**

RIGHT: **3 July 1996. 'WIMBLESONG. Sir Cliff Thrills Centre Court Crowds in Rain'** (*The Sun*).

RIGHT: The musical *Heathcliff*, with songs written by Sir Tim Rice and John Farrar, finally opened in October 1996. Helen Hobson played Cathy.

BELOW: Visiting Haworth Moor, the setting for Emily Brönte's novel *Wuthering Heights*, which Cliff studied as a schoolboy.

90s

HEATHCLIFF
CLIFF RICHARD

'90s

RIGHT: Themed fancy-dress parties held in his gardens including 'Country and Western' (1993), 'Over the Top' (1991), 'International' (1995 – Cliff is on the left of the photograph), 'Woodlands' (1992) and 'Uniforms and Gowns' (1989).

BELOW: The swimming pool at Cliff's current home in Weybridge.

'90s

RIGHT: With his trusted professional and recording manager David Bryce, who has been with him for over 30 years.

ABOVE: 15 January 1996. At the launch of *UK Action*, a Tear Fund initative to alleviate poverty in Britain.

ABOVE: In Portugal with his charity and press affairs manager, Bill Latham, and Bill's girlfriend Jill Clarke.

BELOW: A reunited Cliff and the Shadows, with Hank Marvin, Brian Bennett and Bruce Welch.